Traveling In Thailand
By Coloring

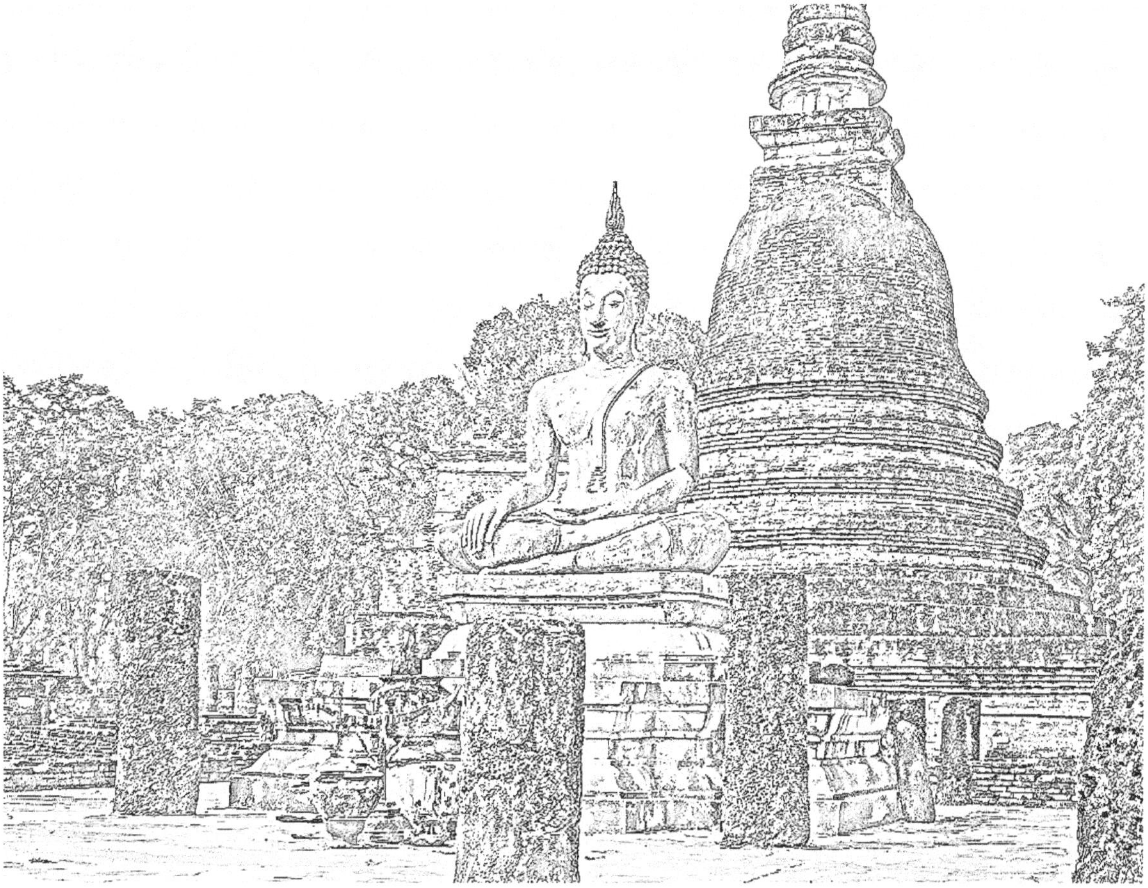

William B. Lewis

Mandala : Traveling
In Thailand By Coloring

ISBN-13: 978-1534952317
ISBN-10: 1534952314

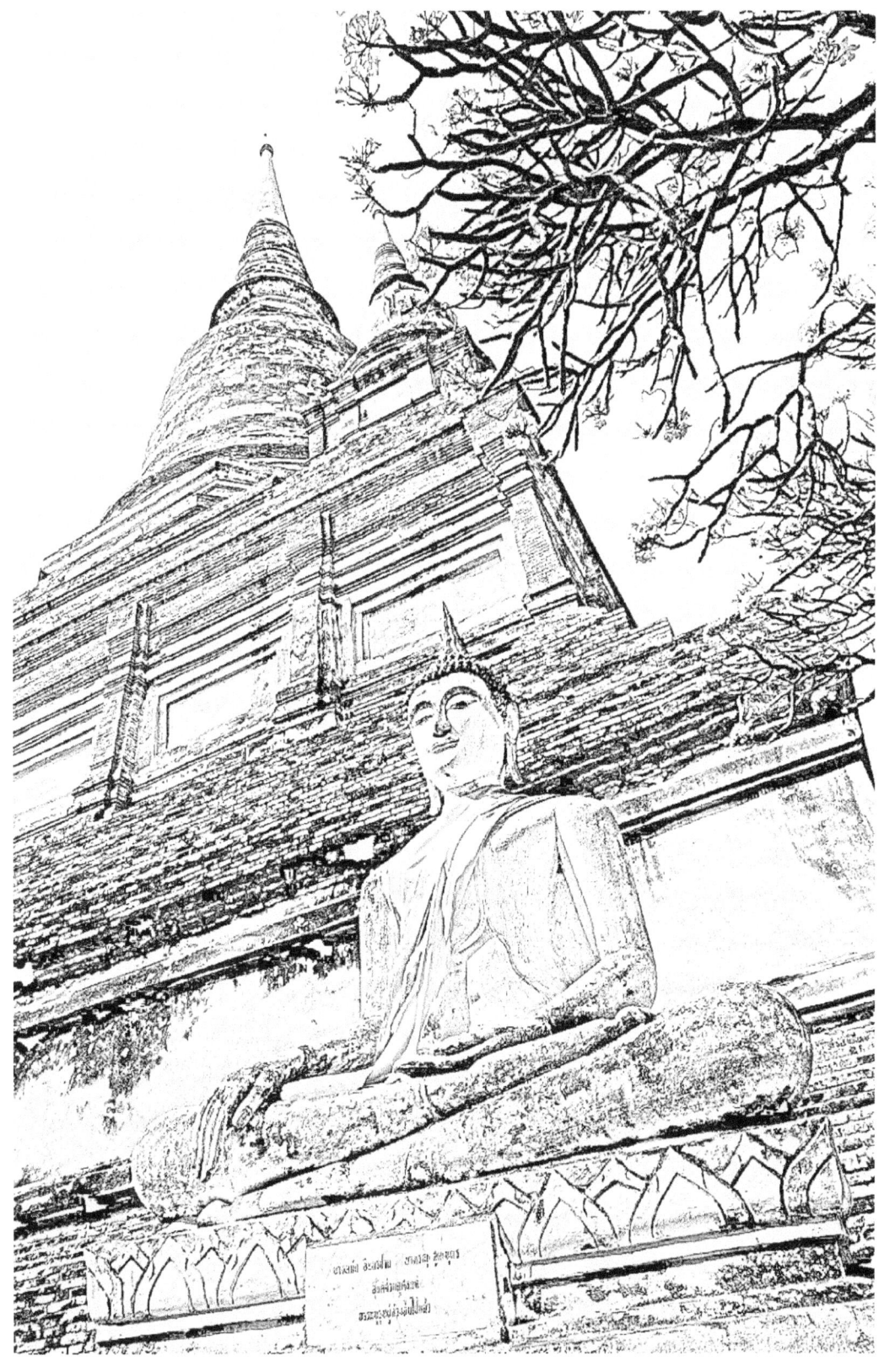

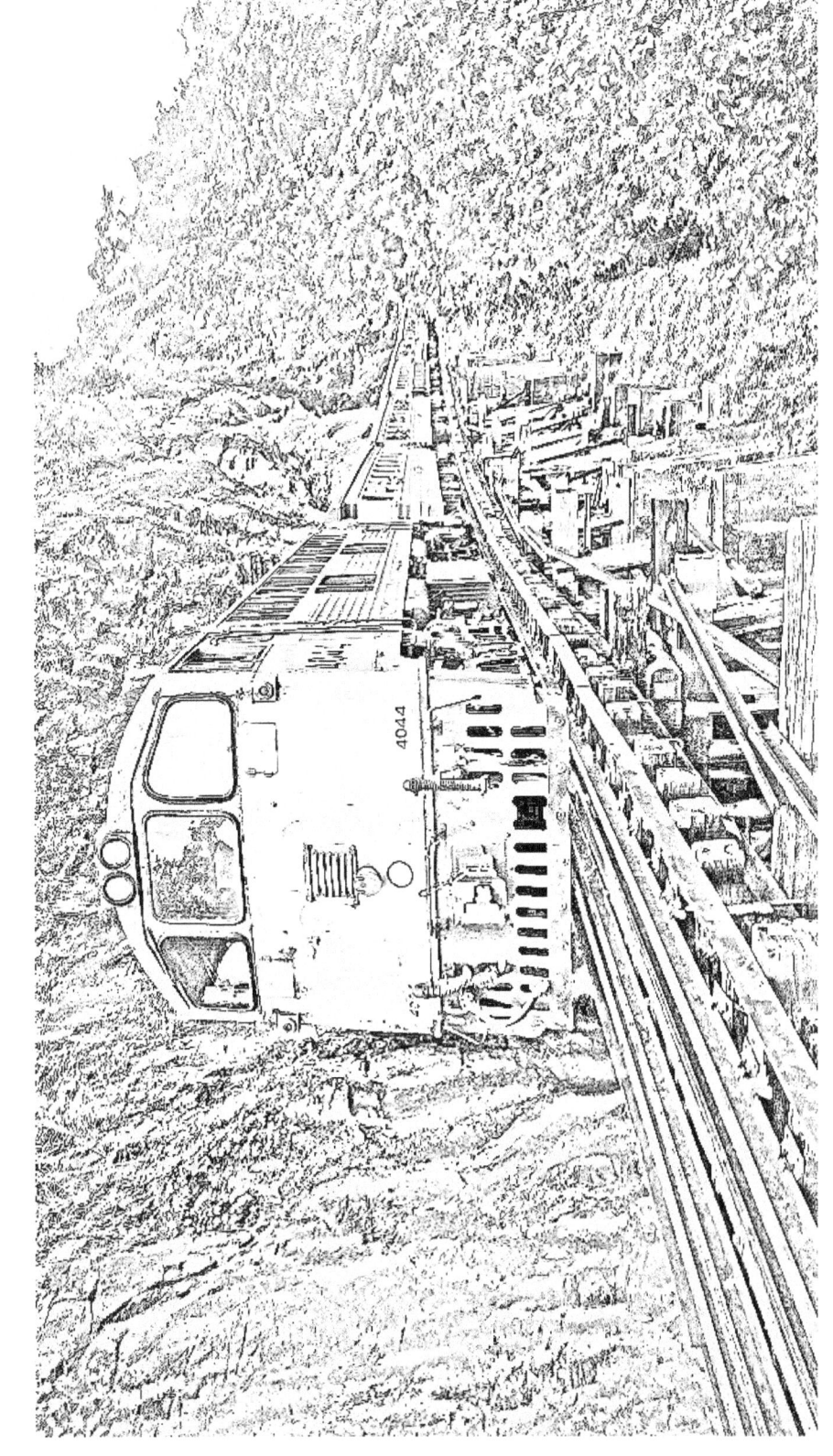

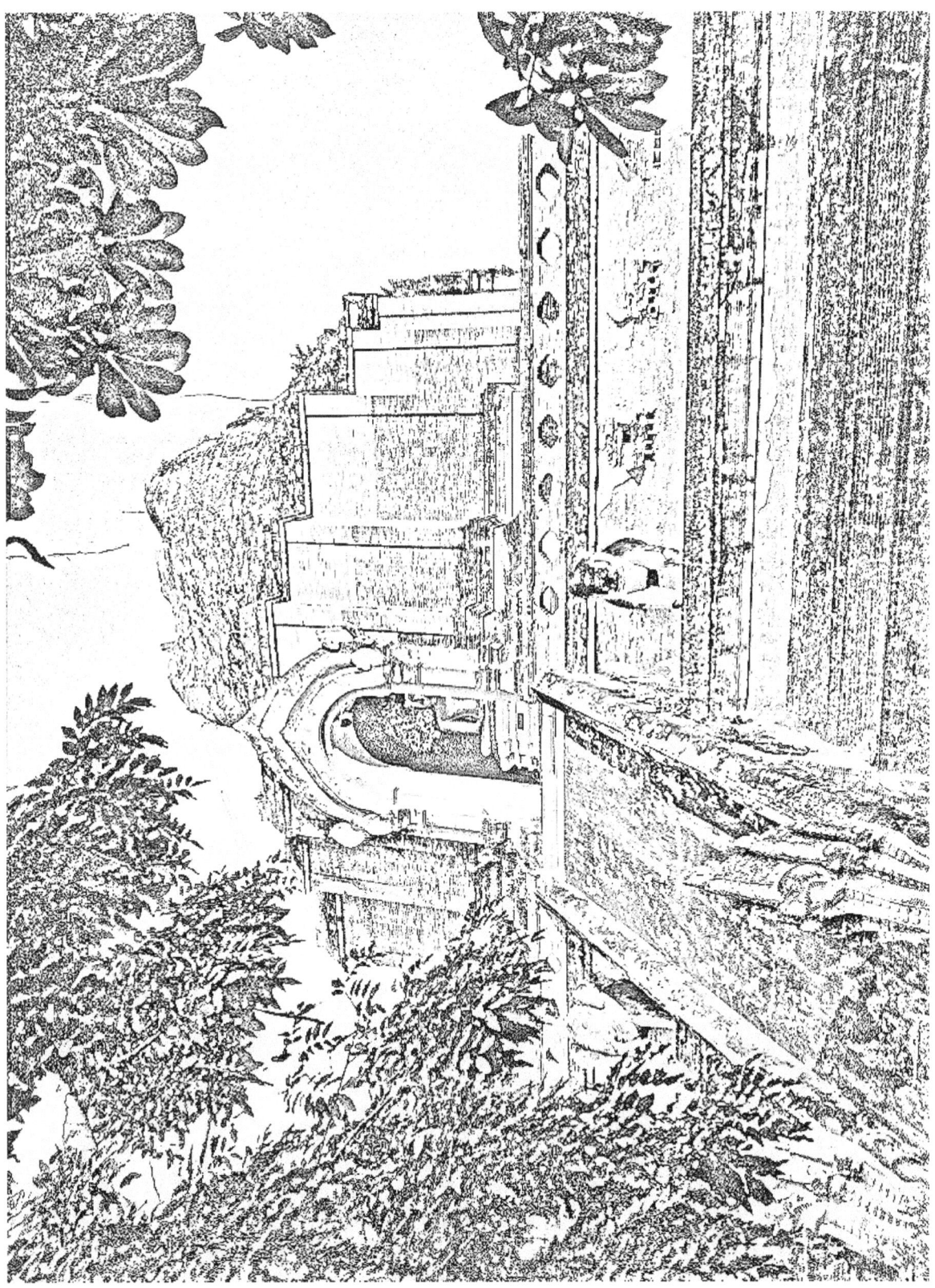

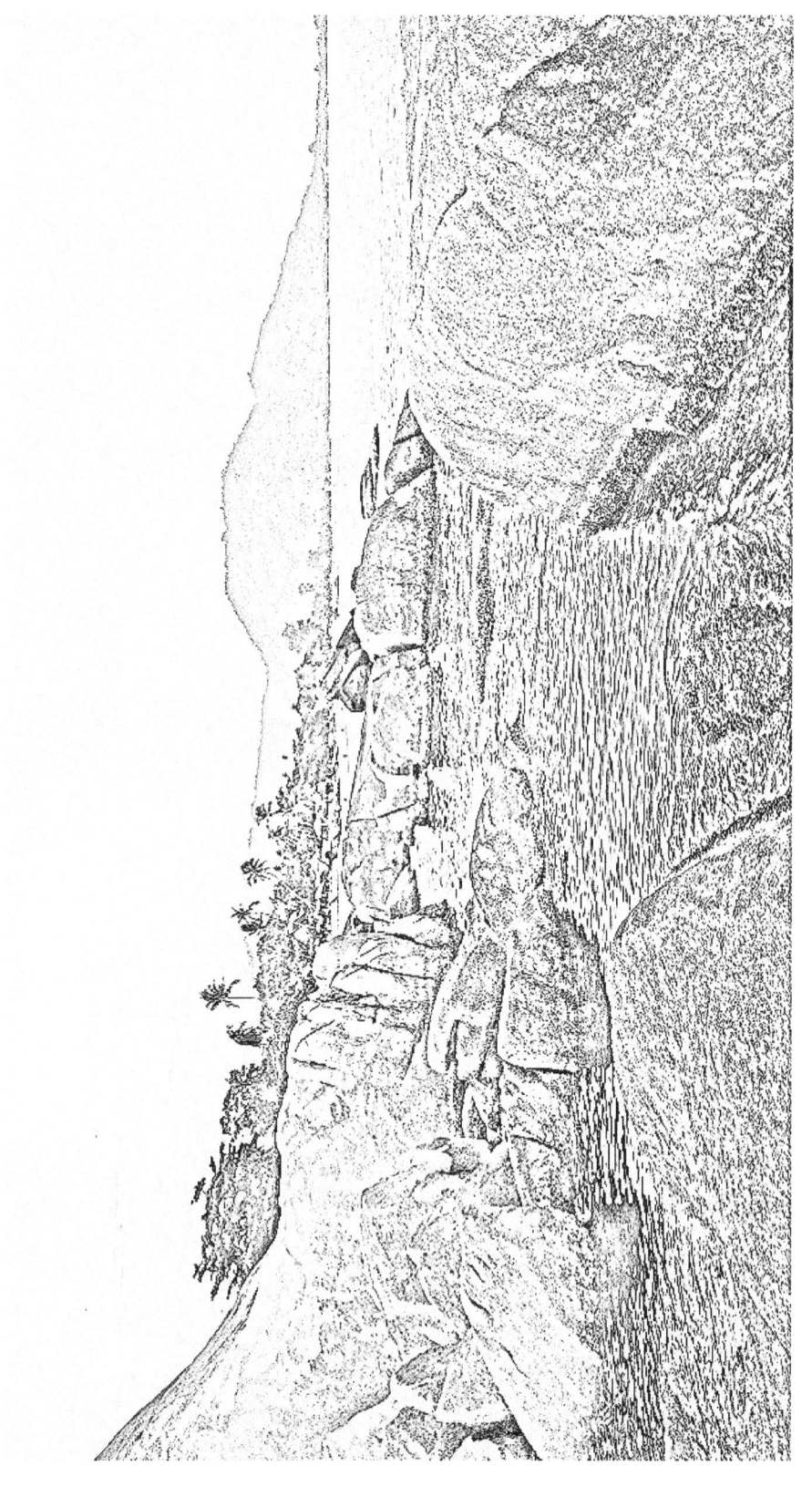

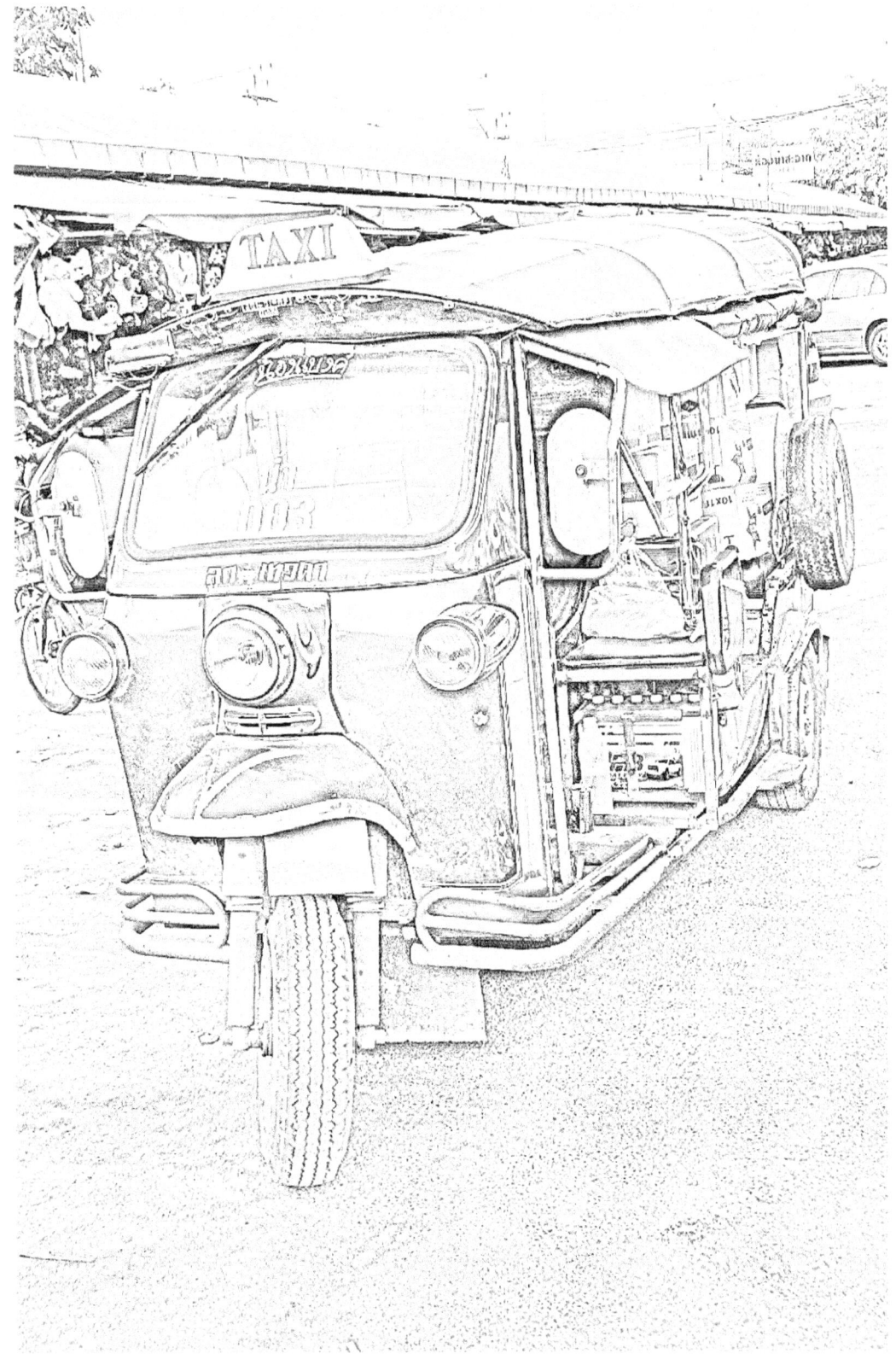

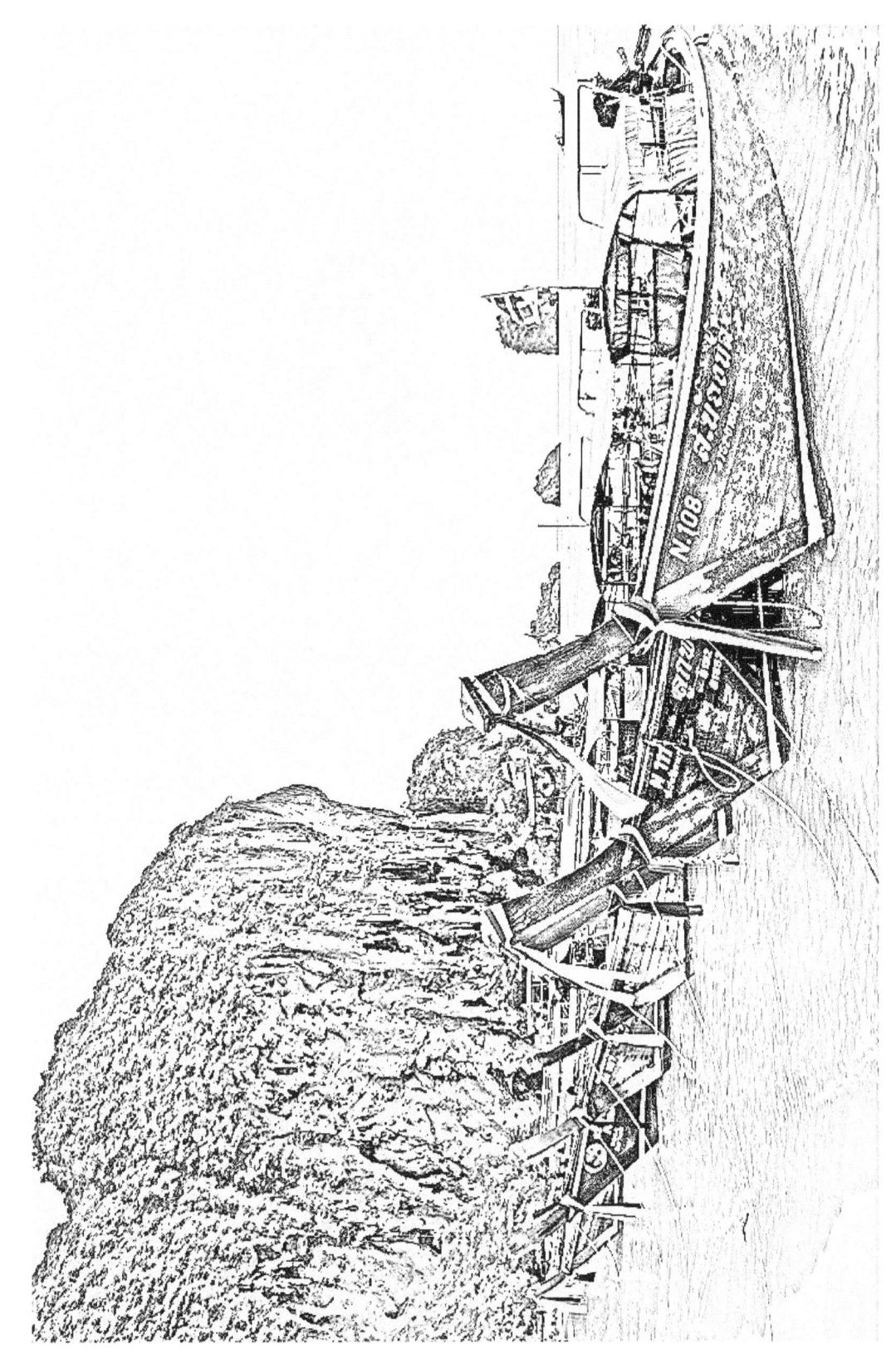

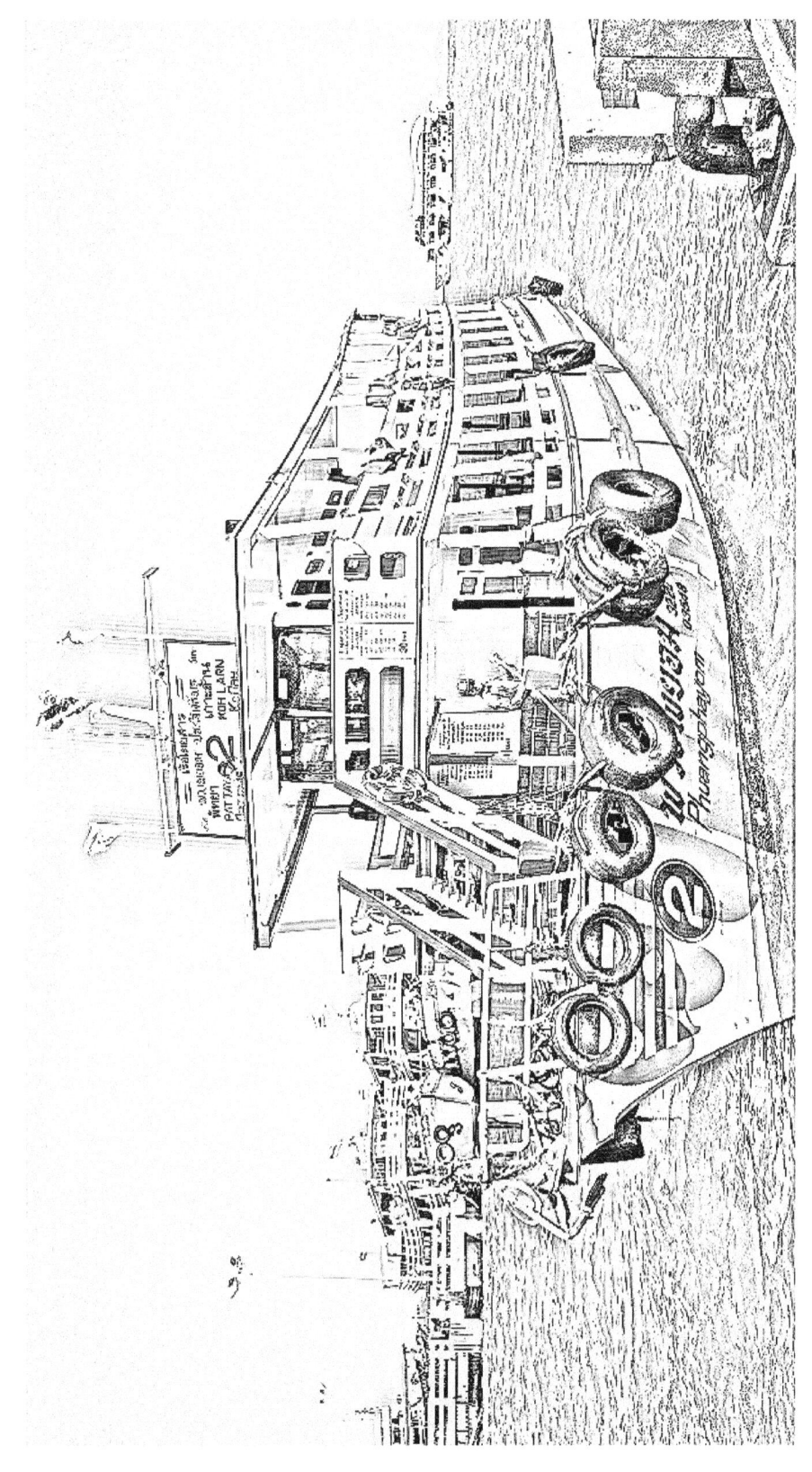

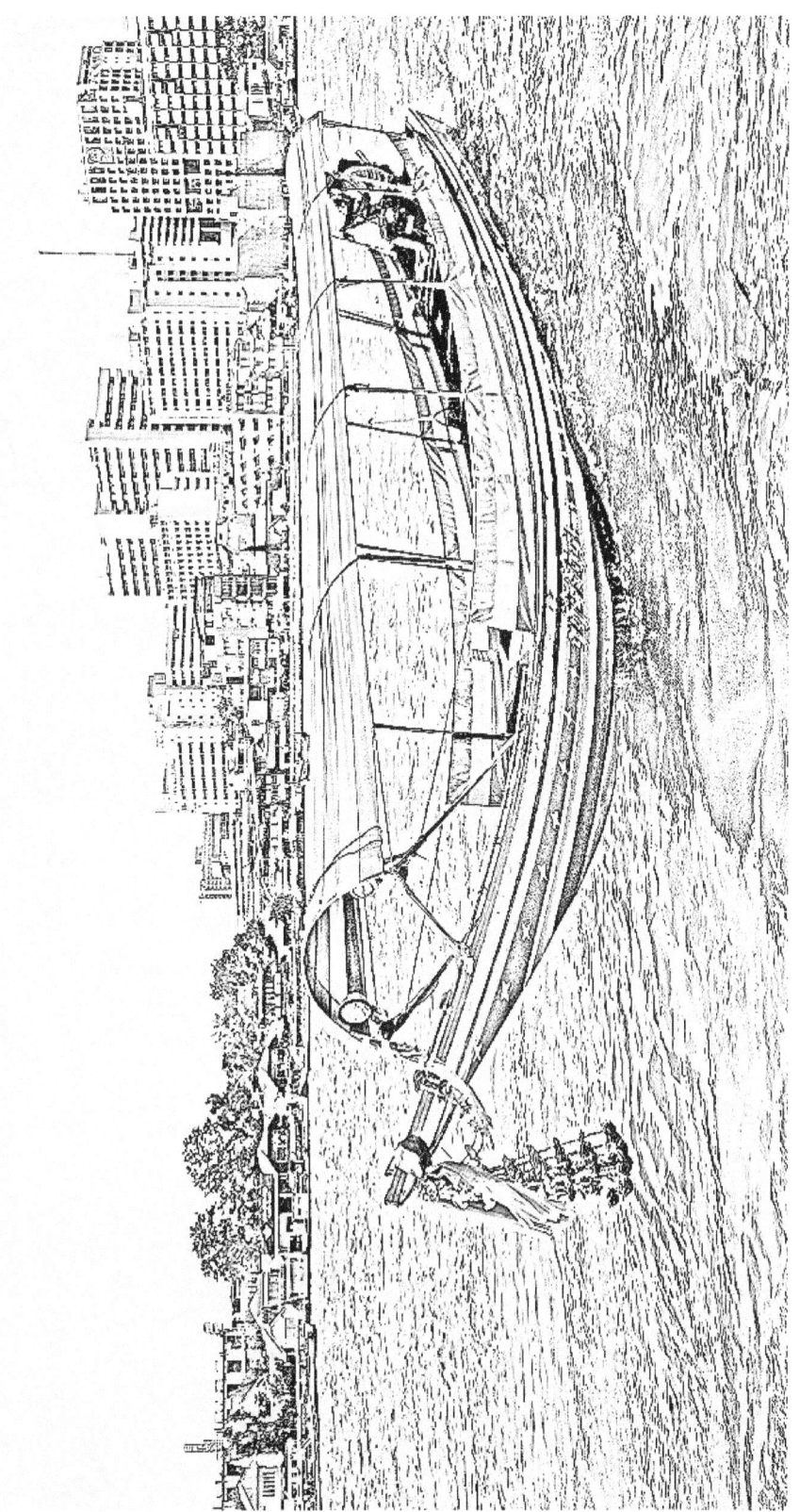

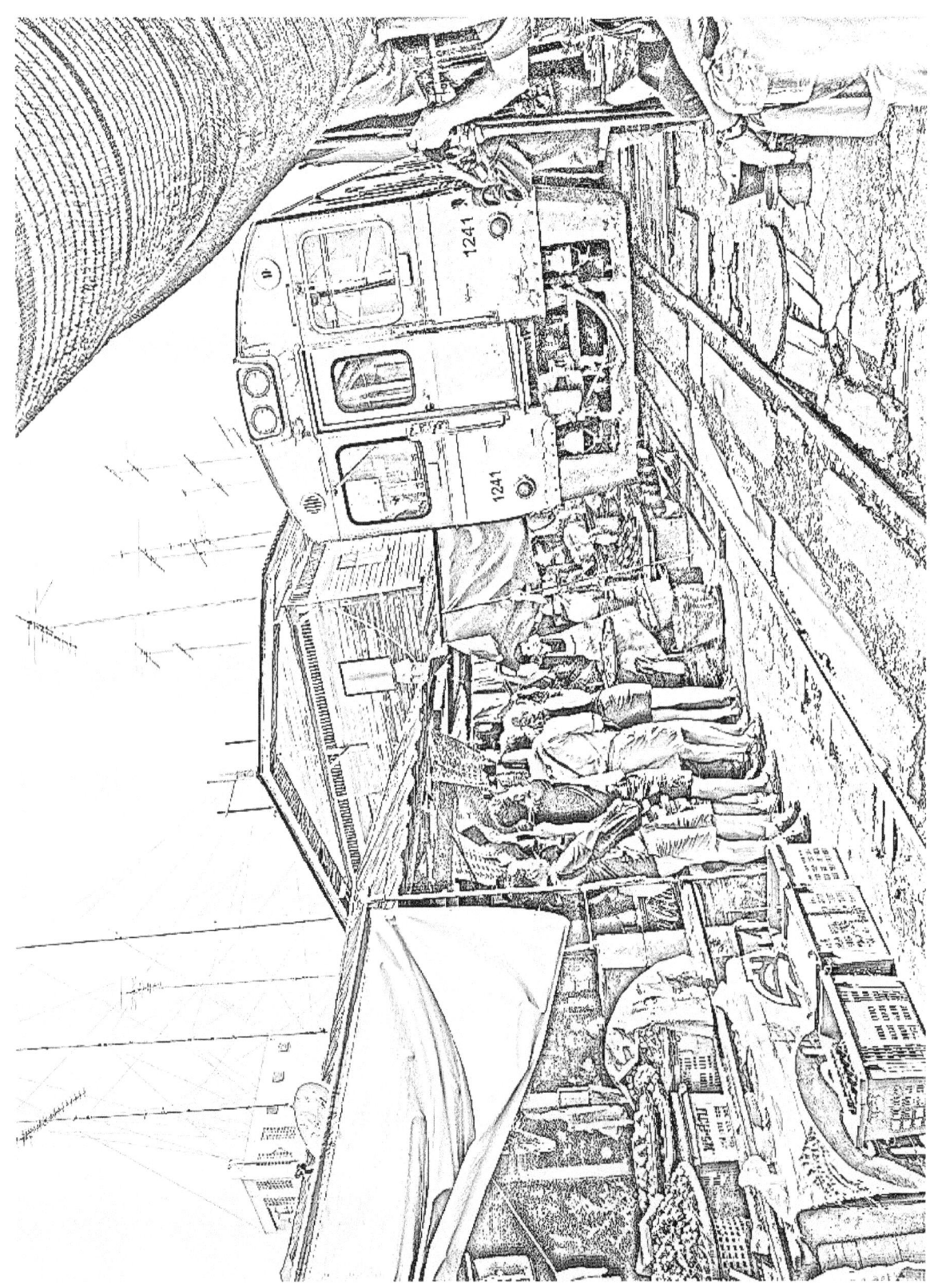

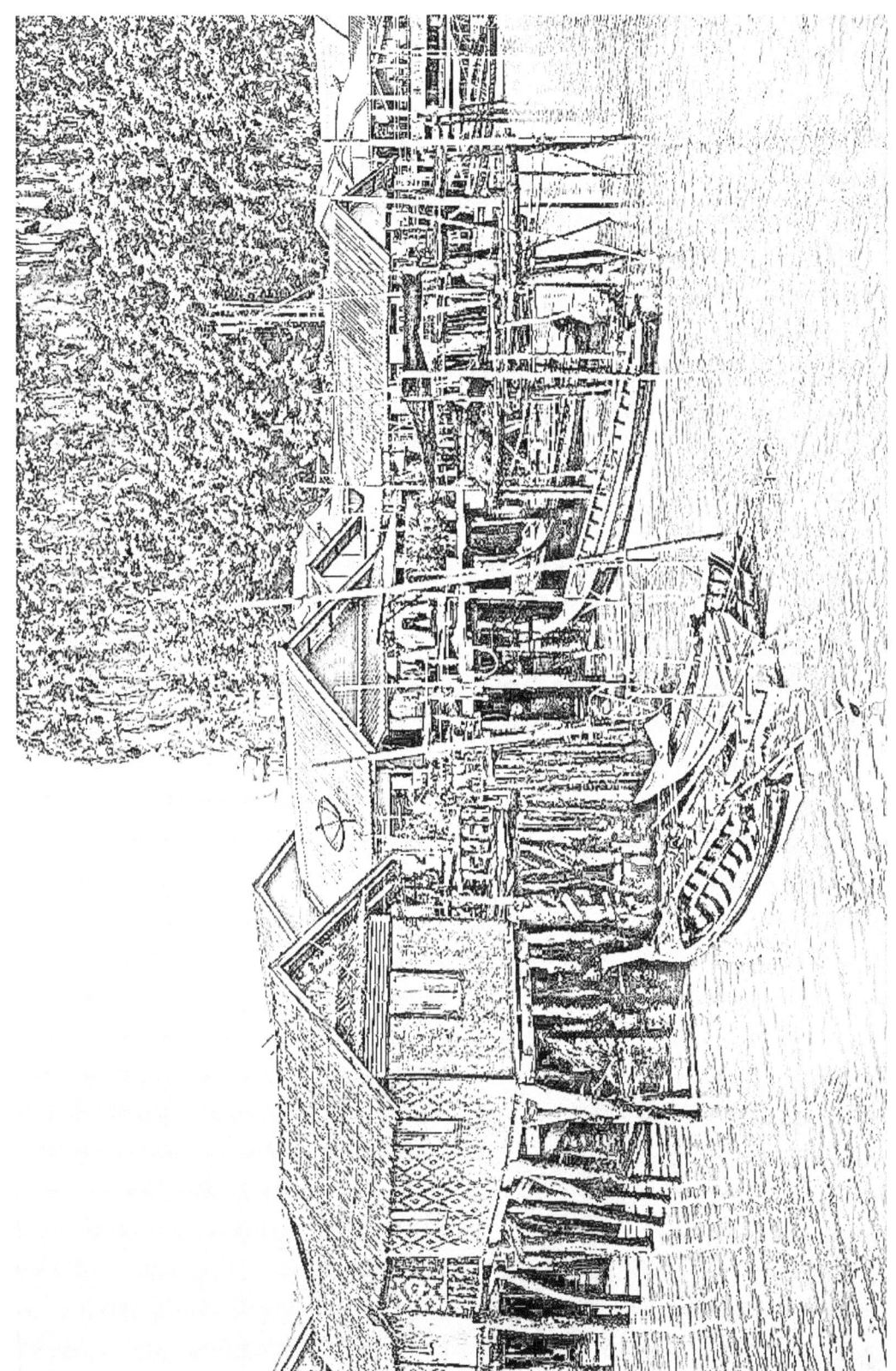

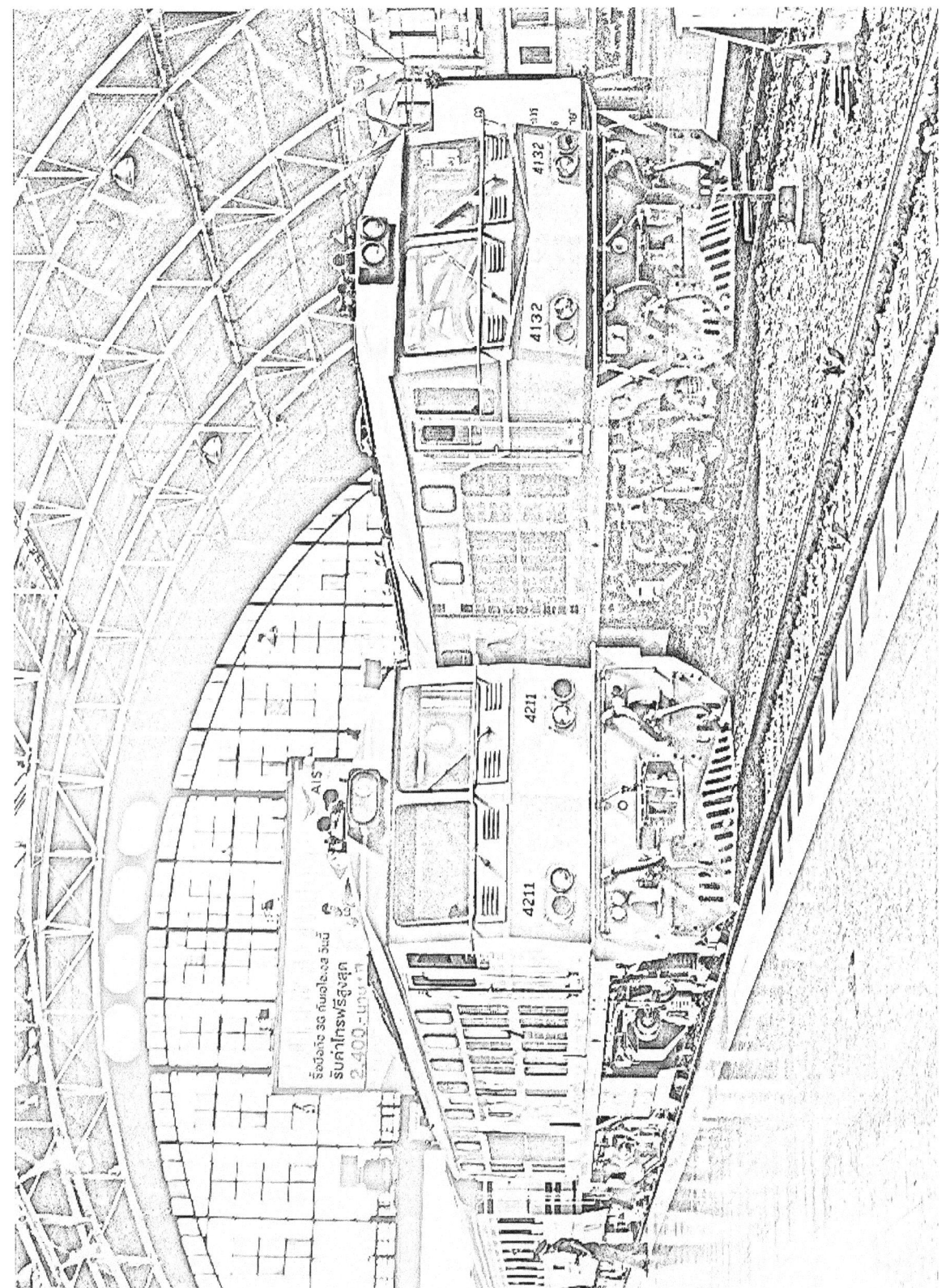

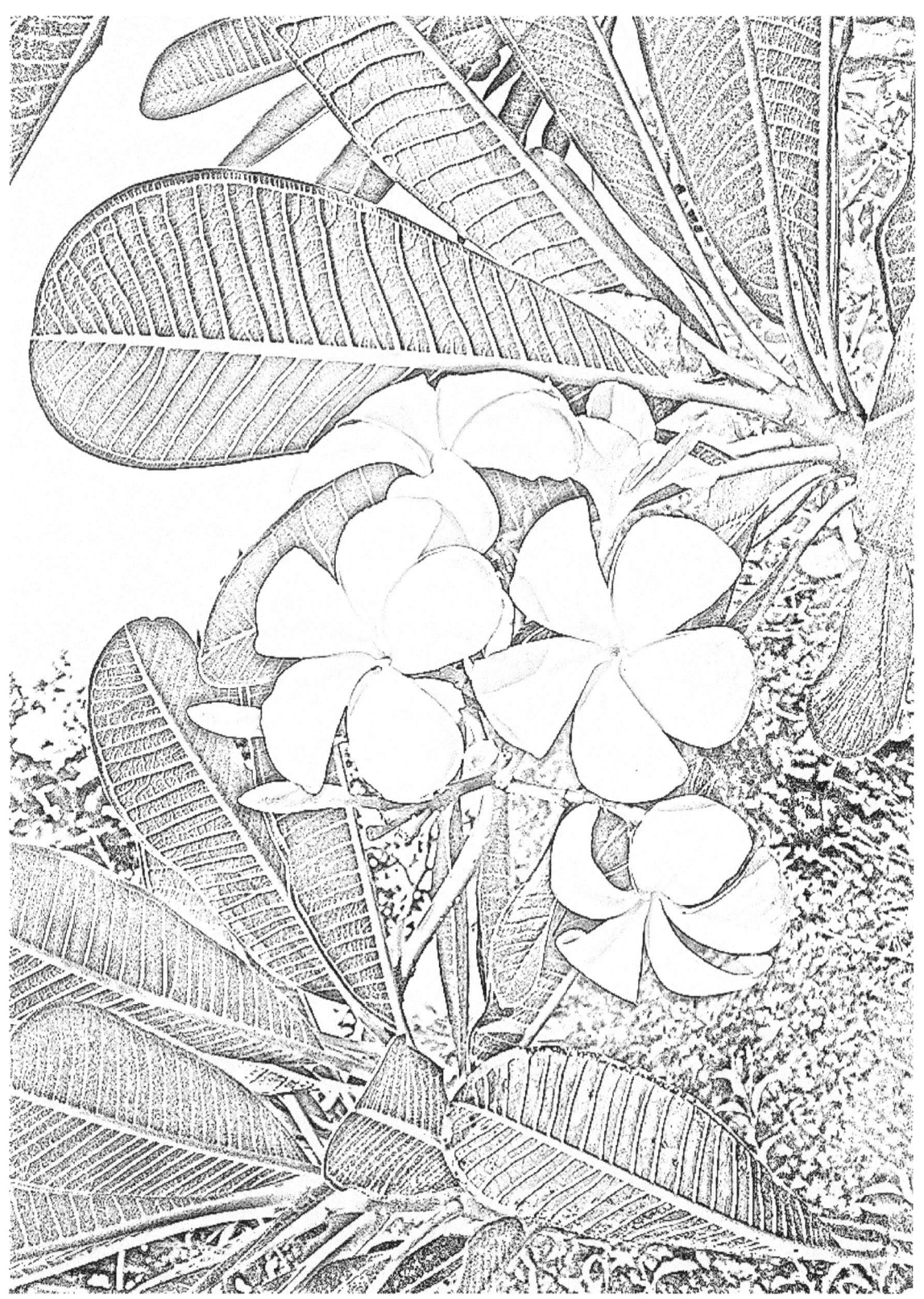

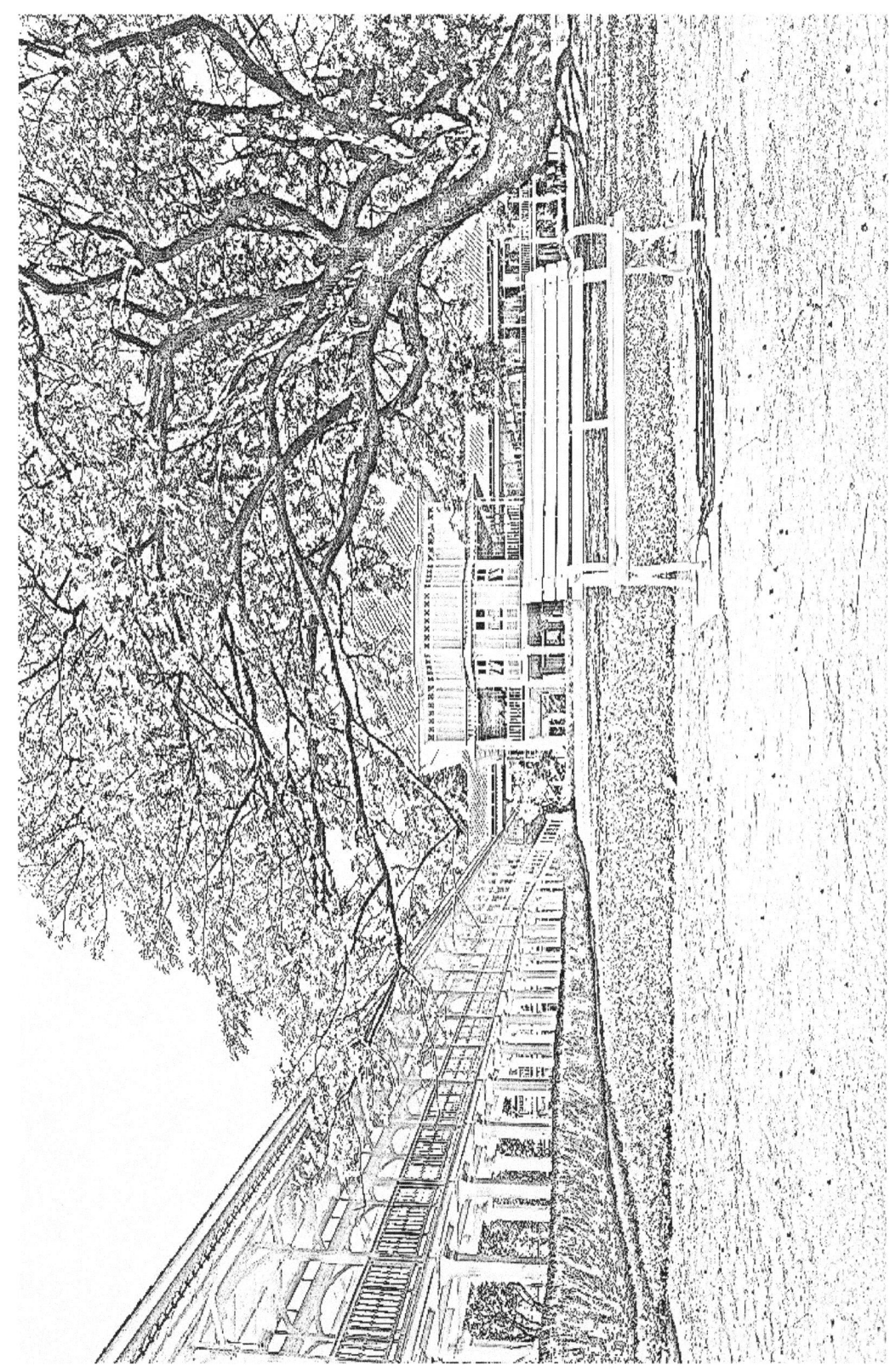

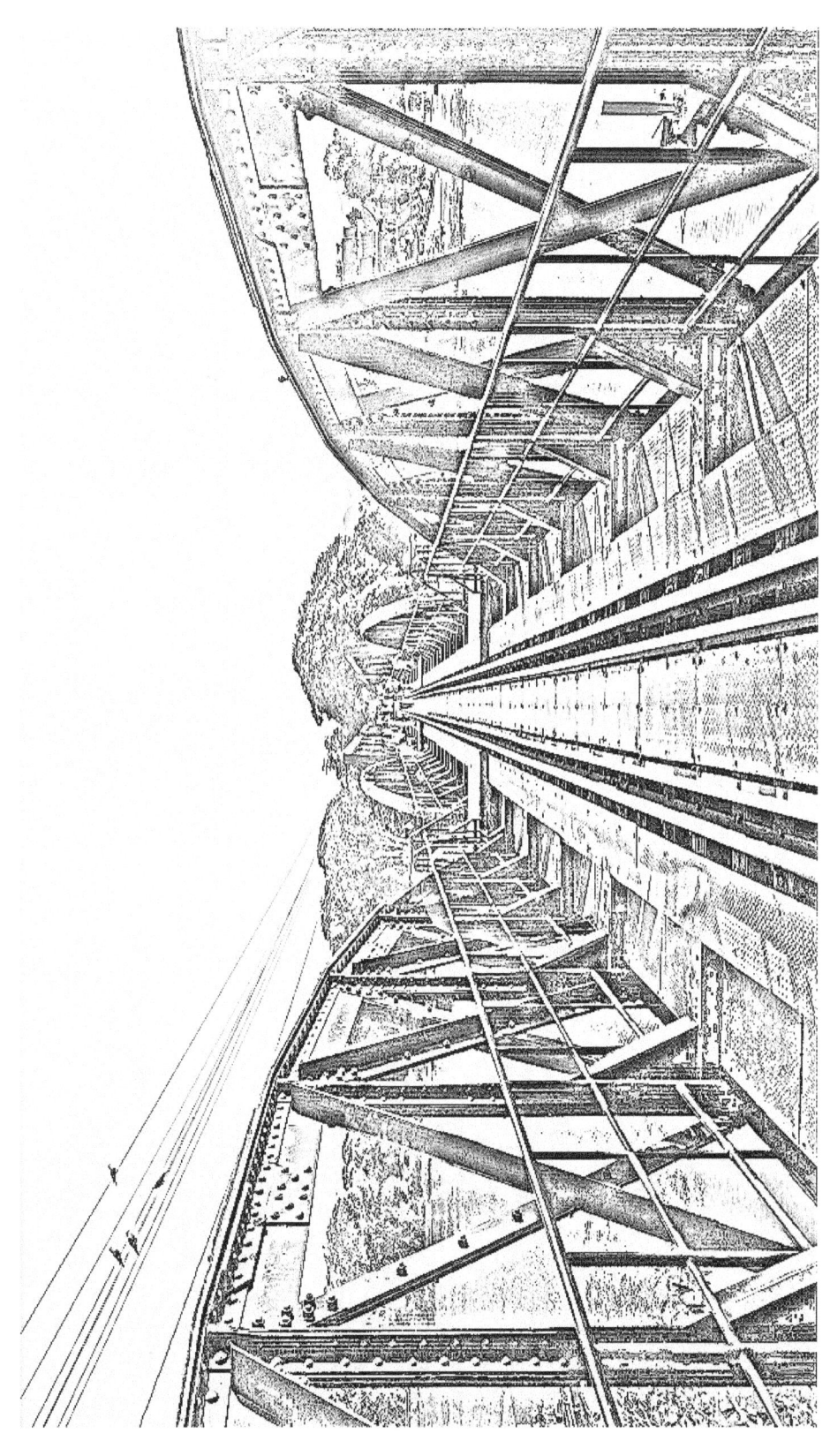

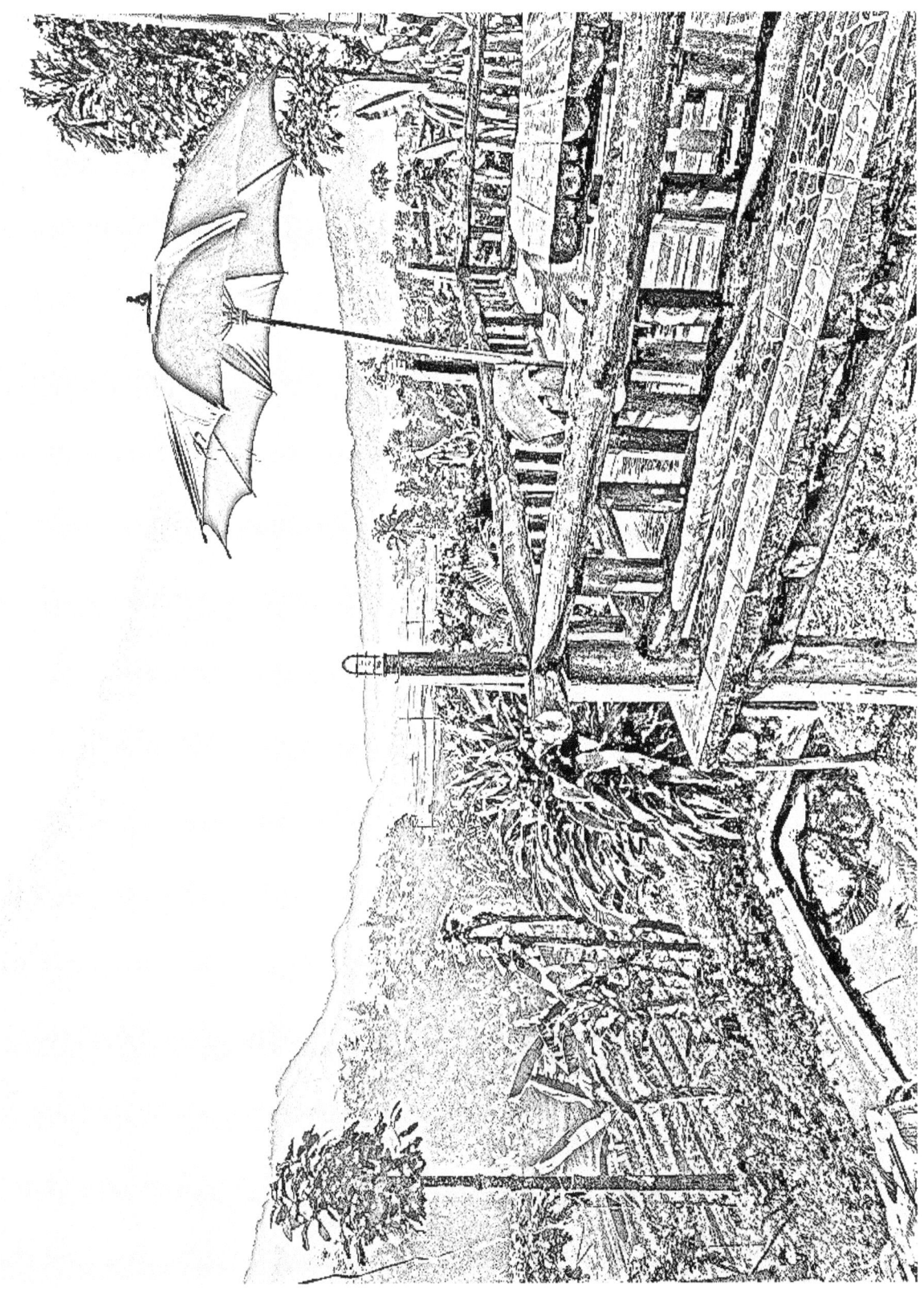

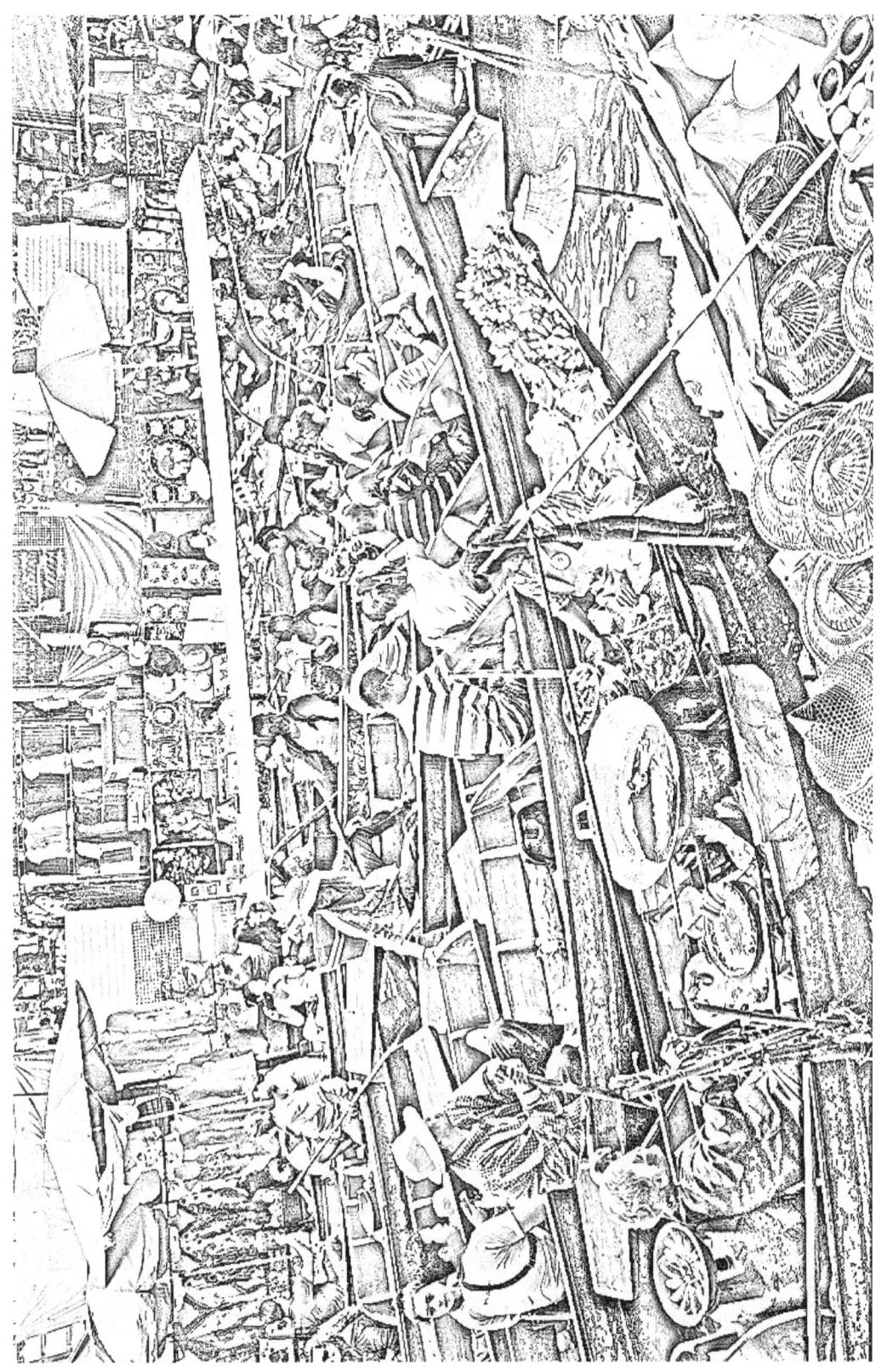

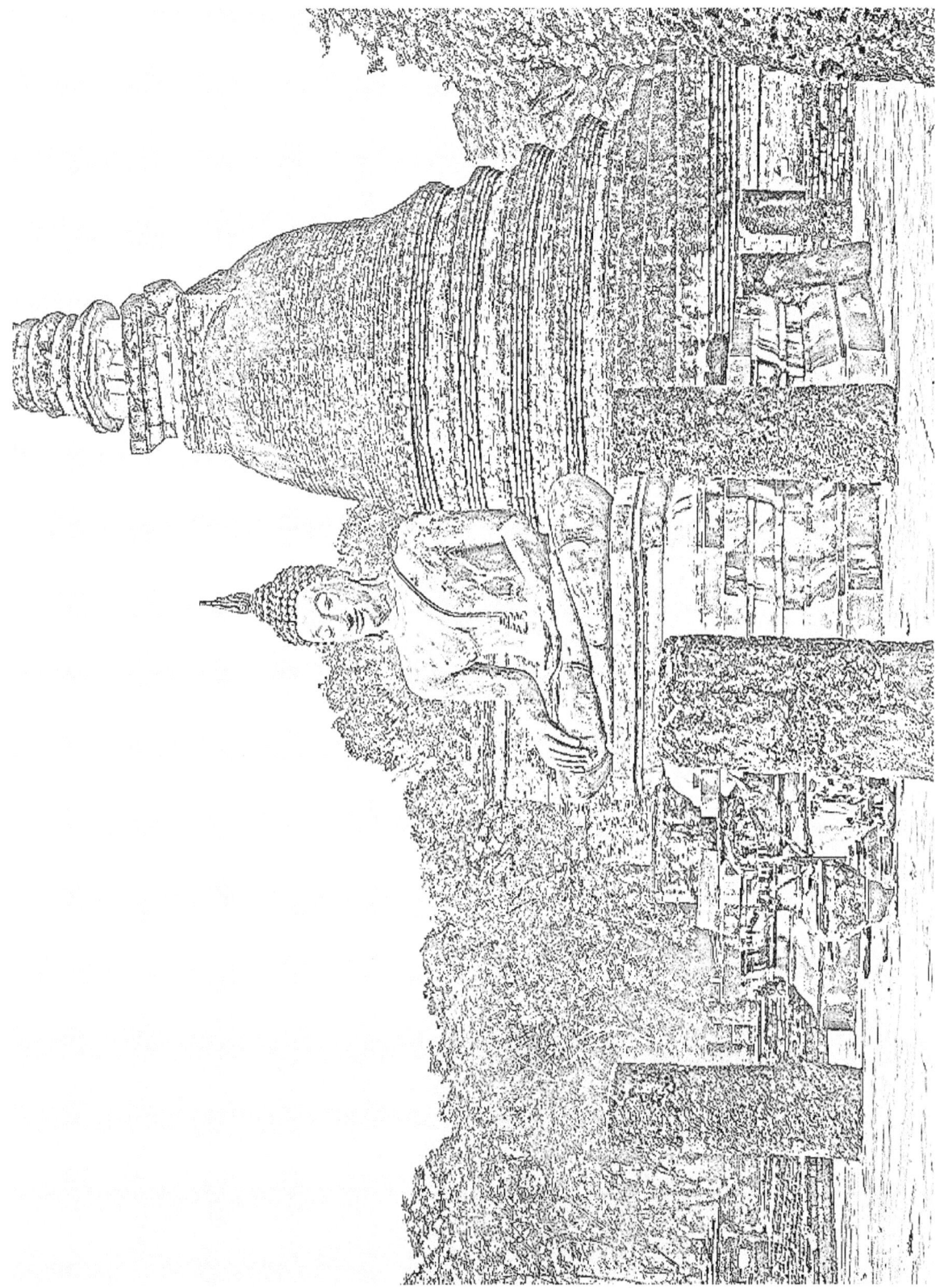

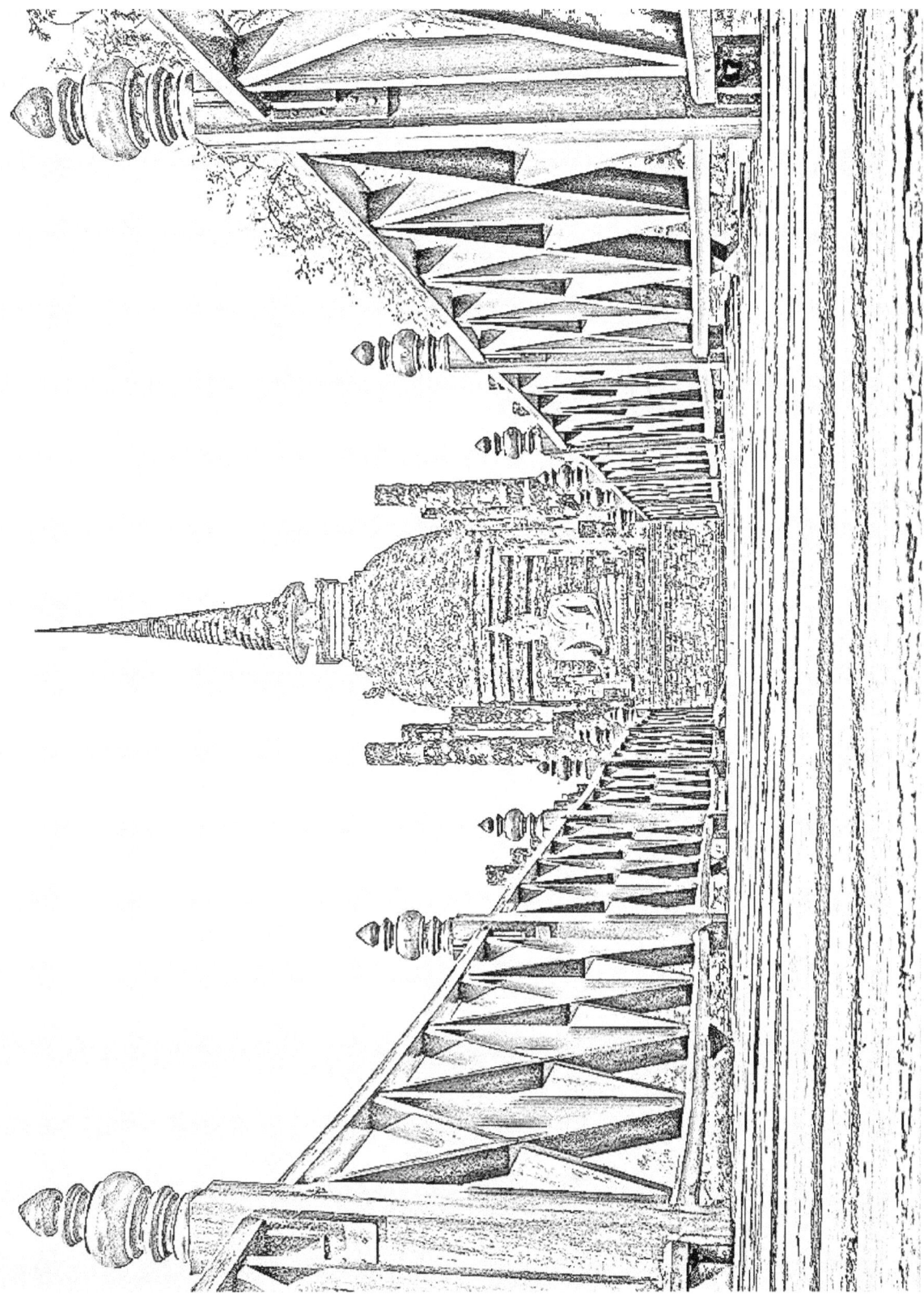

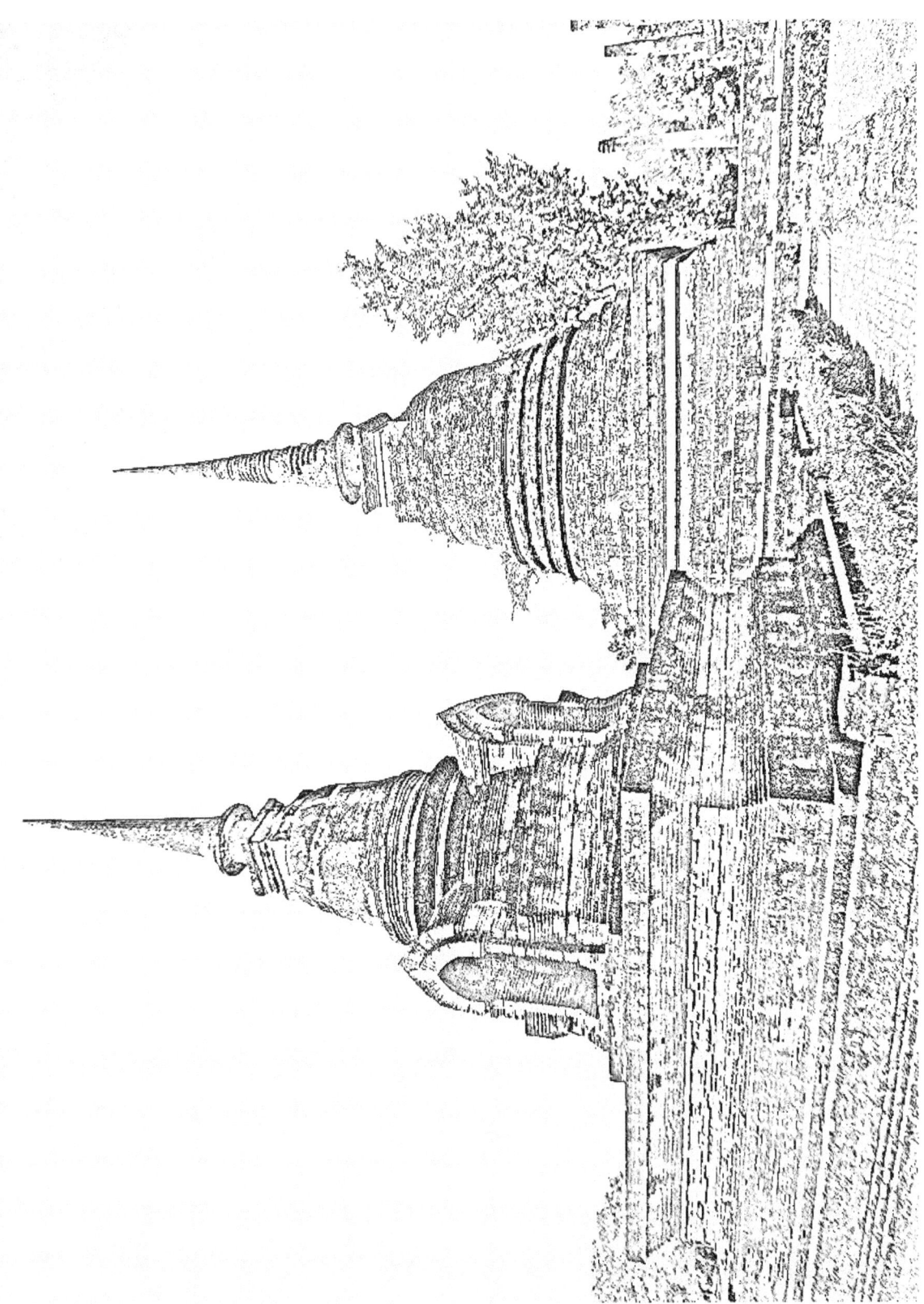

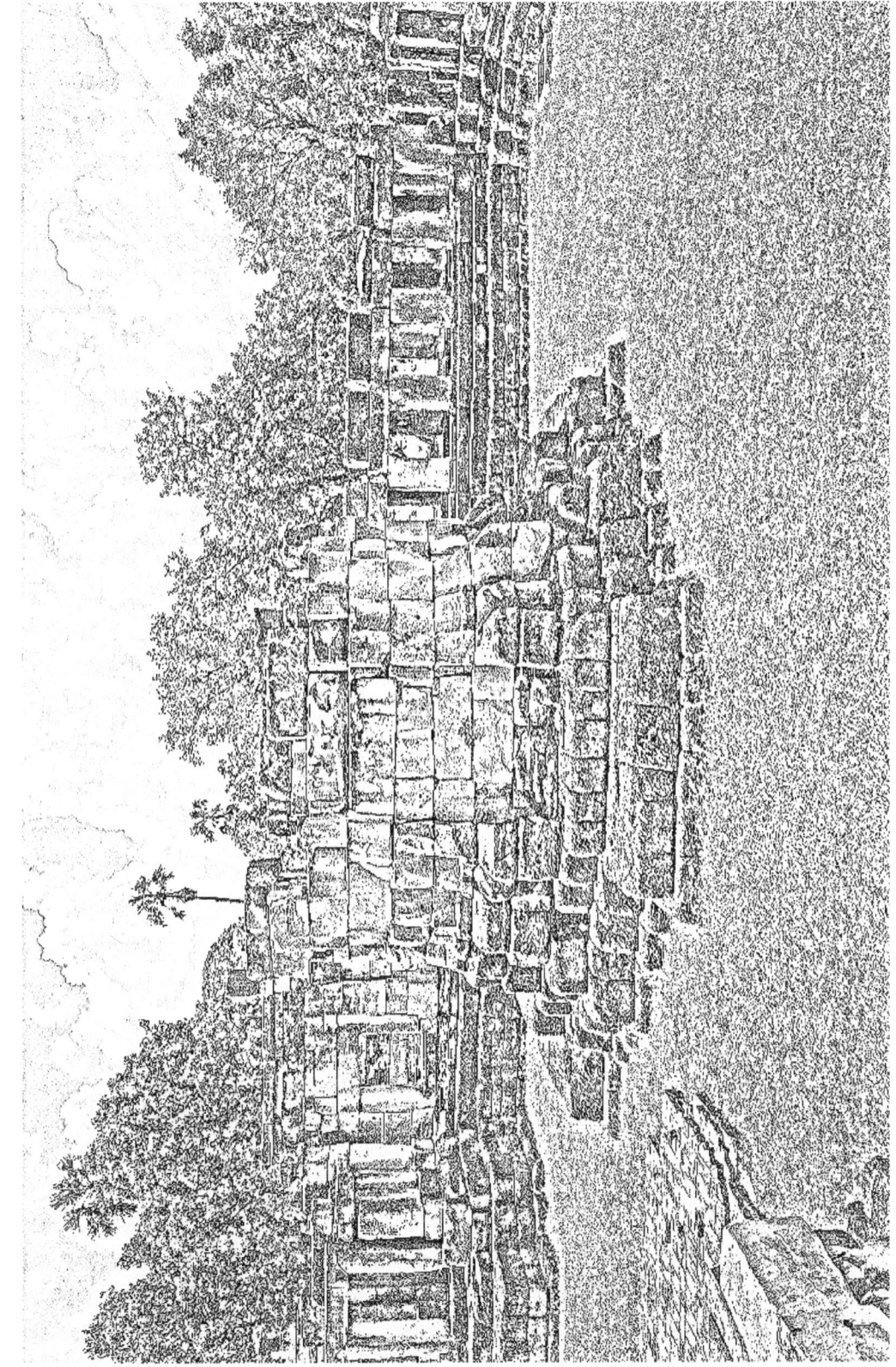

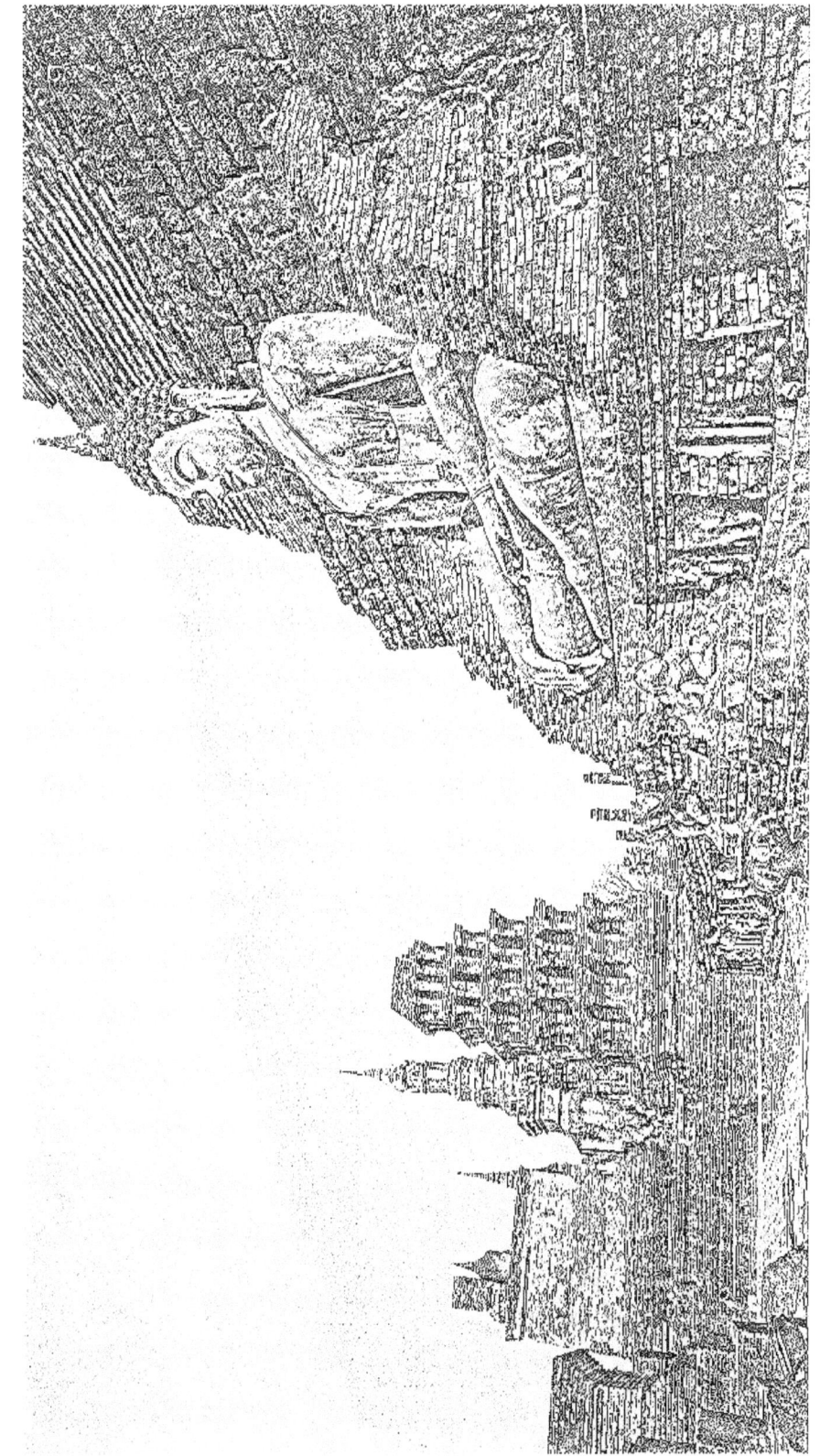

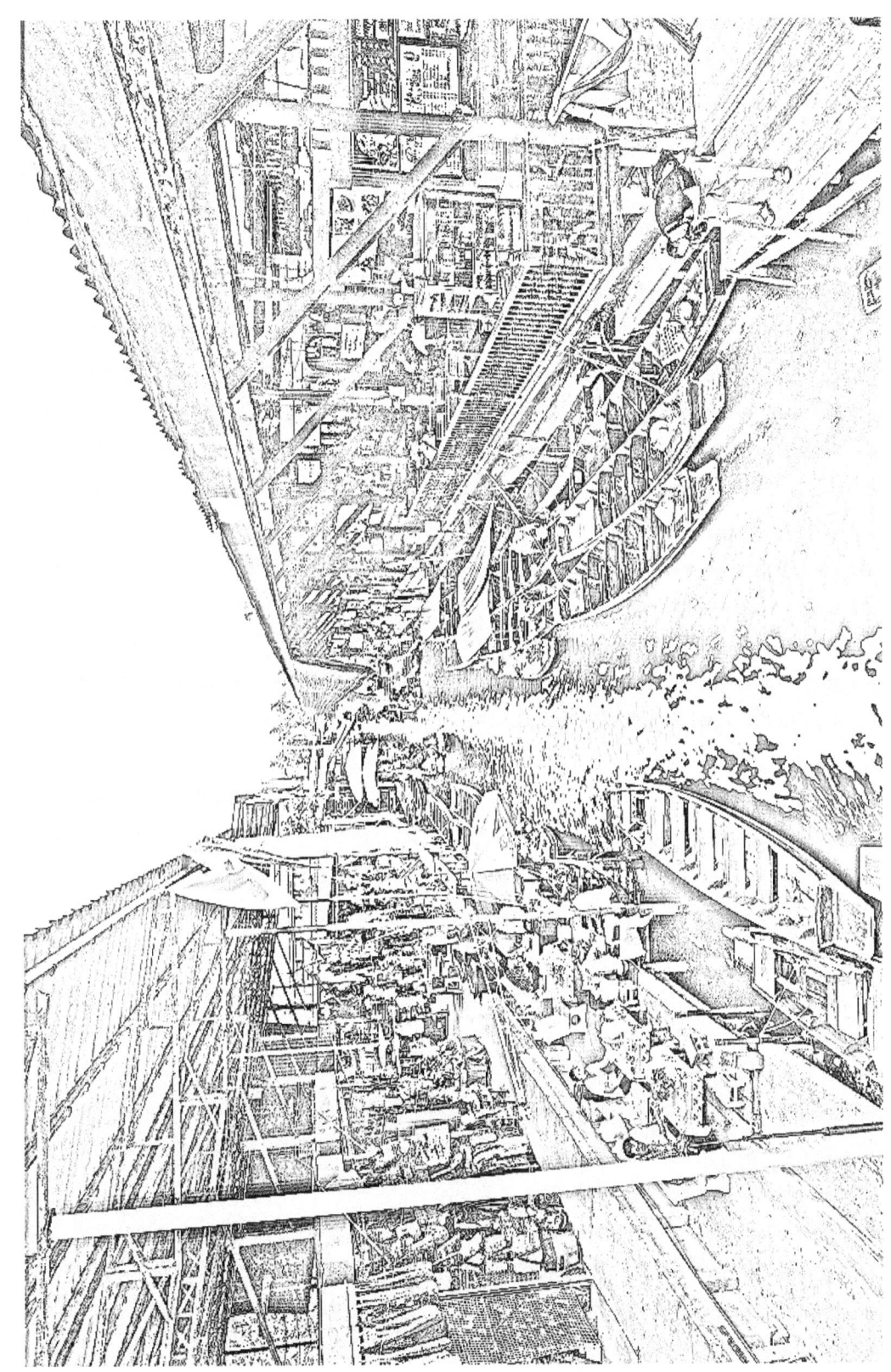

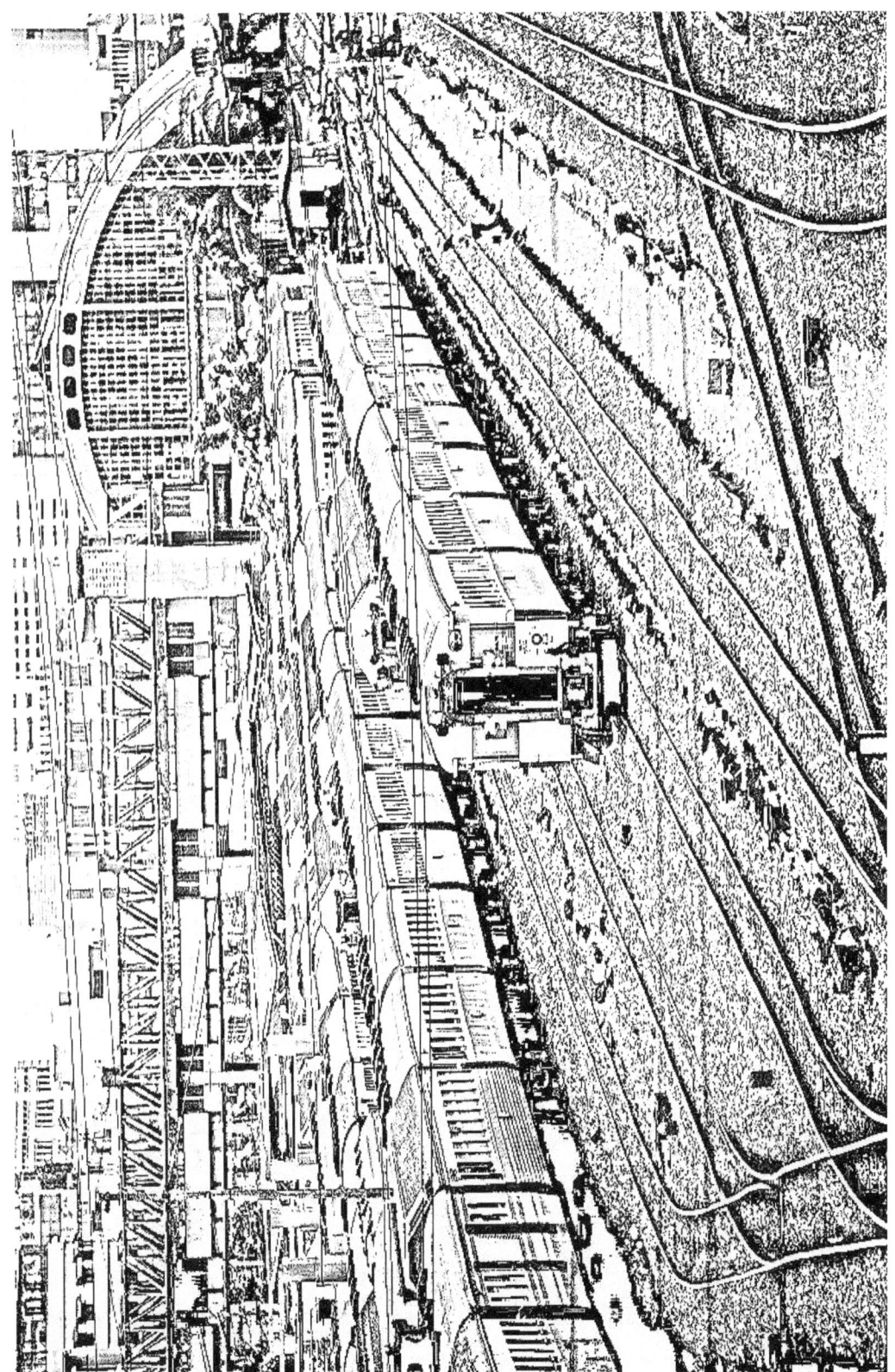

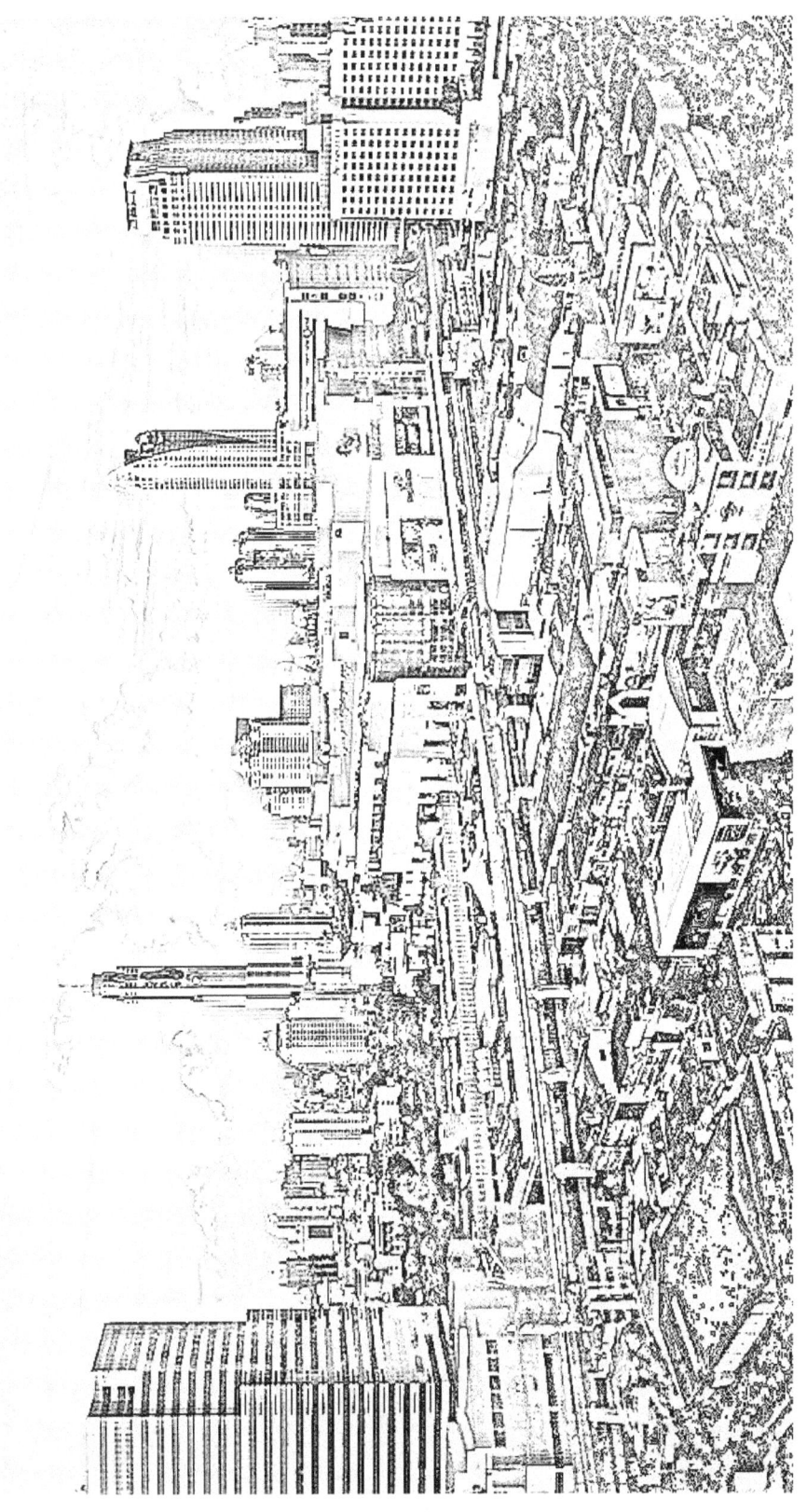

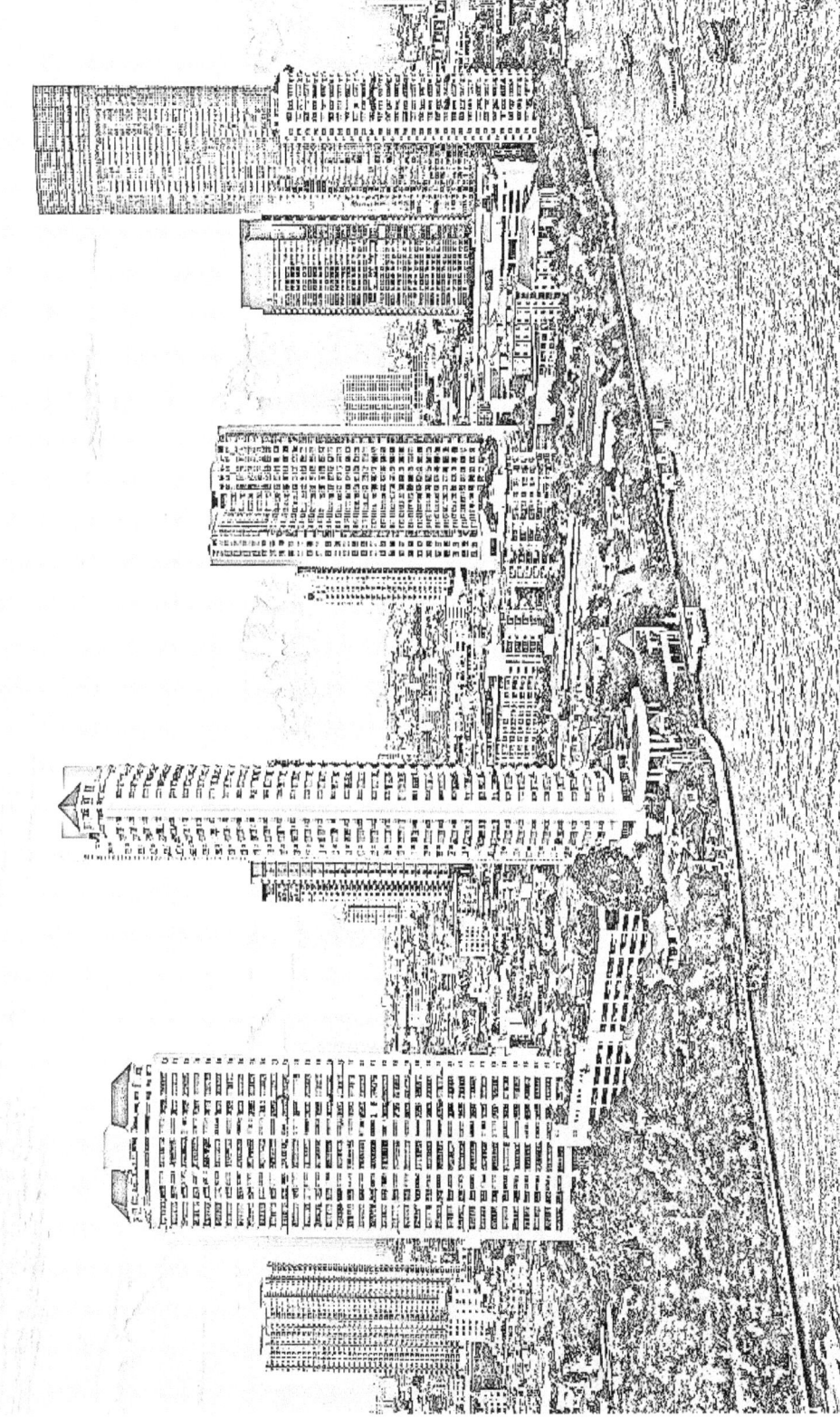

Thank you

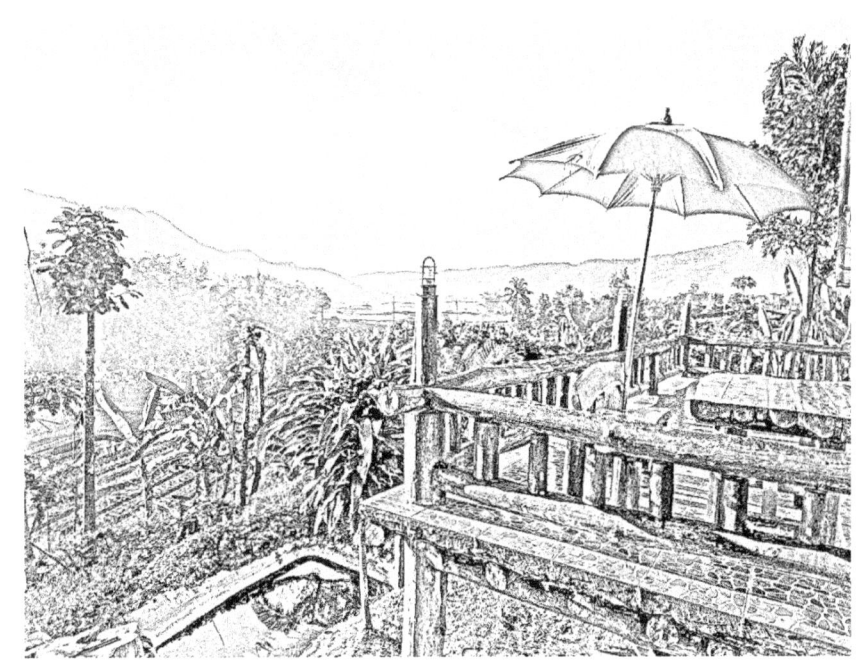

www.ingramcontent.com/pod-product-compliance
Lightning Source LLC
Chambersburg PA
CBHW080634190526
45169CB00009B/3388

* 9 7 8 1 5 3 4 9 5 2 3 1 7 *